YOUR KNOWLEDGE HAS VALUE

AF135871

- We will publish your bachelor's and
  master's thesis, essays and papers

- Your own eBook and book -
  sold worldwide in all relevant shops

- Earn money with each sale

Upload your text at www.GRIN.com
and publish for free

Integrity in Schools in Tanzania. Influence of the Integrity of the Principal on Academic Performance of Students in Secondary Schools

A Case Study of Mbulu District

Chelestino Mofuga

Bibliographic information published by the German National Library:

The German National Library lists this publication in the National Bibliography; detailed bibliographic data are available on the Internet at http://dnb.dnb.de.

ISBN: 9783346256270
This book is also available as an ebook.

© GRIN Publishing GmbH
Nymphenburger Straße 86
80636 München

Print and binding: Books on Demand GmbH, Norderstedt, Germany
Printed on acid-free paper from responsible sources.

The present work has been carefully prepared. Nevertheless, authors and publishers do not incur liability for the correctness of information, notes, links and advice as well as any printing errors.

GRIN web shop: https://www.grin.com/document/924980

INFLUENCE OF INTEGRITY ATTRIBUTE OF HEAD OF SCHOOLS ON STUDENT ACADEMIC PERFORMANCE IN SECONDARY SCHOOLS IN TANZANIA, A CASE STUDY OF MBULU DISTRICT

Author: Dr Chelestino Simbalimile Mofuga:

ABSTRACT

This study assessed the influence of the integrity attribute of the school leaders on the student academic performance in the secondary schools. Explanatory cross-sectional survey design with a concurrent mixed approach using quantitative and qualitative data were employed. A total of 202 teachers used to provide evidence on heads of school's integrity in influencing students' academic performance using questionnaires, in-depth interview and focus group discussion. The collected data were analysed using SPSS version 23 for quantitative data, and thematic analysis for qualitative data. Significant relationship between integrity and students' academic performance was revealed. The study concluded that integrity attribute significantly influences positively the students' academic performance Therefore, the study recommends the government to allocate enough funds for professional development for the aspirant of head of secondary schools and review educational policy on the training and development of teachers before and after appointment into headship post.

KEY WORDS: Integrity, leadership, Academic performance.

Index

ABBREVIATIONS:

HoS   Head of school

FGDs   Focused group discussion

SPSS   Statistical Package for Social Scientists

RCC   Regional consultative meetings

NECTA   National Examination Council of Tanzania

SD   Standard Deviation

SDA   Strongly Disagree

DA   Disagree

NT   Neither disagrees nor agrees

AG   Agree

SA   Strongly agree

INTRODUCTION

The concept of integrity in education context is of paramount importance for educational institutions like schools prosperity. Integrity attribute can be regarded as principal and muscles of any organization intended to improve performance and sustainability of the institution through running effectively and efficiently. Duggar, (2015), states that integrity comprises of characteristics of an individual that are consistent, considerate, compassionate, transparent, honest and ethical status. Integrity is related with keeping promises and keeping thrust, respect and responsibility (Turknett, 2007). Therefore, the current study seeks to explore ways to improve student academic performance through integrity.

The study used mixed method quantitative and qualitative approaches with mixed concurrent explanatory cross -sectional survey questionnaires, to explore efficiency of the integrity of Head of schools on the student academic performance in Mbulu District. There six attributes of integrity, accountability towards individual and society, clean, efficient, and trustworthy and access of information. According to Najib, (2009), these attributes can create harmony, transparency services in workplace and will help contribute to the development of the secondary schools and improvement in leadership and administration, which in turn leads to good academic performance of students. In the present context where the government emphasizes the human model of the country in terms of intellectual knowledge, expertise and skills, integrity also plays a important role of component in improving the robustness of the educational performance model. Integrity is a contributor to the recognition of lives enriched by work and relationship in secondary schools.

In particular, integrity is deemed as a vital component as it is fundamental to the functioning of private as well as public secondary schools. Integrity reduces external regulations (Najib, 2009 and sidek, 2009), enhances cooperation with stakeholders, strengthens stakeholders confidence in secondary schools (Mahathir, 2001), and diminishes conflict (Hubert et al, 2007). In contrast, working without integrity, such as the occurrence of misunderstanding, fraud and corruption can result in enormous financial losses, severe reputational damages and bankruptcy (Sidek, 2009). Integrity is a concept of consistency of actions, values, methods, measures, principles, expectations and outcomes that connotes a deep commitment to do the right thing for the right reason, regardless of the circumstances (Hopkins, 2012).

In context of individuals, integrity plays important roles that reflect the ability of the individual (Head of school) in performing assigned tasks in educational management, particularly in secondary schools. Integrity acts as the foundation of characters that describes an individual as an honest person in every area of his or her life. Meanwhile Hidalgo (2007) stated that integrity acts as guidelines, a benchmark, and a point of references or a goal that is used to make decisions that rely on truth and honesty. A study by Else bower, (2013), clarified the functions of integrity as appositive attribute that is fundamental for leadership. Therefore, it is imperative that leaders, lead with integrity, honesty, and values, should be concerned with individual wholeness and conscience, have the quality of being true to oneself and recognize that it is essential to maintain personal and professional relationship.

Leadership has a classical and vast history which associates many researchers work with it because there is an assumption that leaders are not born (Aline and Ramkumar, 2018), they can be developed (Darling-Hammond et al., 2007; Ardichvili, Dag, and Manderscheid, 2016). According to Northhouse (2007), leadership is a process of an individual to influence group(s) of individuals towards attainment of a common goal. Moreover, Swanson and Holton's (2001) defined leadership as application of expertise that is a combination of experiences, problem-solving skills, and knowledge in achieving a stipulated objective. Consequently, in the twenty-first century, a significance of leadership for successful operation of secondary schools had been widely acknowledged (Bennis and Naus, 2003).

Fundamentally, academics stand as a branch of education (Feather, 2016). While academics literally is knowledge especially on theoretical perspectives one gets by attending secondary school education, the later means inculcating the knowledge, moral values and positive thinking (Abubakar, 2018). According to Annie, Howard and Mildred (1996), academic performance is the outcome of education or the extent to which a student, teacher or institution has achieved their educational goals. Academic performance is measured by the final grade earned in the course. The Divisions are used as a convenient summary measure of the academic performance of secondary schools' students in Tanzania. The Divisions are better measurement because it provides a greater insight into the relative level of performance of individuals. Basically, various studies have applied such measurements in combination (Ismail, 2016).

Likewise, Mbulu district has been struggling to improve school facilities to facilitate effective teaching and learning (RCC, Manyara Report, 2016) and the report shows that the district has surplus facilities and infrastructures for schools, compared to other districts in the country, yet the performance is poor, for instance, the NECTA results for 30 secondary schools from 2014 to 2018 were as follows: Division, I was 131, division II was 889, division III was 1684, division IV were 5012 and division 0 were 3087 students for just five years. Therefore, students got division four and zero 5012 and 3087 respectively are regarded as failures because they can't proceed with advanced level studies (NECTA, 2014, NECTA 2015, NECTA, 2016, NECTA, 2017 and NECTA, 2018). To accomplish this study focused into the following objectives:

1. OBJECTIVES OF THE STUDY

1.1 Main objective

To assess the influence of integrity attribute of Head of Schools on the student's academic performance in selected Secondary schools in Tanzania.

1.2 Specific objectives

In order to address the general objective, the study sought to accomplish the following three intertwined specific objectives:

i. To assess the influence of accountability attribute of Head of schools on the student academic performance in selected secondary schools.
ii. To assess the influence of honesty attribute of Head of schools on the students' academic performance in selected secondary schools.
iii. To assess the influence of efficiency attribute of Head of schools on the students' academic performance in selected secondary schools.

2. METHODOLOGY

To address the research objectives mixed research approach was opted. This allowed the use of explanatory and cross-sectional because it meticulously describes the influence of integrity attributes on students' academic performance using data collected at one point in time. Thus, this design cannot gauge the temporal variations or a trend in the data collected (Kothari, 2009). Moreover, the survey design was selected because of its aptness in obtaining the obligatory quantity of data in running quantitative analysis as Hair *et al.*, (2006). A survey can also be standardized to allow an easy comparison of results (Nyamsogoro, 2010). Furthermore, the explanatory survey is an effective tool for getting a cause-effect relationship (Ghauri and Gronhaug, 2005) and the results can be generalized to a large population. As a result, the quantitative findings of this study were generalized to the whole Manyara region, and to the country, Tanzania. Qualitative approach is more in-depth and holistic than quantitative, generating rich materials on which to base the findings of a piece of research

Qualitative methods were used to supplement the findings to obtain views, attitudes, and personal perceptions, which are termed as personal constructs (Shek, 2012). Qualitative research methods, unlike quantitative methods are best able to take account of the nature of human perceptions, thoughts and ideas, which recognize the complex and dynamic quality of the interpersonal world (Salmon and Rickaby, 2012). Given the ethics, integrity, perpetual, interpersonal and relational nature of organizational performance, a qualitative approach to this study is highly appropriate in order to yield relevant insights (Thomas, 2002). Qualitative research was conducted to 237 teachers from public and private secondary schools. The data were analyzed using thematic content analysis and emerging themes and sub themes from constructs were elicited and compared to the literature of integrity and performance. The approach identifies commonalities and differences in qualitative data, before focusing on relationship between different parts of data, thereby seeking to draw descriptive and or explanatory conclusions clustered around themes.

A total sample size of 237 was used, which was obtained using the formula developed by Yamane (1967), which was calculated as follows;

$$n = \frac{N}{1 + N(\ell)^2} \quad ....equation3.1$$

Where, $n =$ Sample size, $N =$ Population size with certain characteristics and $\ell =$ Precision factor coefficient (5%). This is also termed as the desired margin of error (ME) expressed as a proportion. According to Krejcie and Morgan (1970) and Tejada and Punzala (2012), this formula is simple and gives a high degree of accurate sample size, also fits with the available parameter N. Therefore, according to the formula:-

$$Sample(n) = \frac{583}{1 + 583x(0.05)^2} = 237 ....equation3.2$$

$$n = 237$$

3. FINDINGS AND DISCUSSION

Influence of Integrity Attribute on the Students' Academic Performance

The results for assessment of the influence of integrity attribute of the heads of schools on the students' academic performance in selected secondary schools in Mbulu district is presented in table 3.1 below. The table 3.1 summarises frequencies and percentages distribution of the 30 items of integrity to show the extent of application of integrity attribute on school leadership and its impact on students' academic performance. The results indicate that the item which says the head of school would steal from the organization scored the highest frequency of 85.70% (sum of 74.80% strongly disagreed and 10.90% disagreed). This means heads of schools cannot steal the school's resources. Therefore, the integrity attribute of trustworthy is possessed and practiced by heads of schools in Mbulu district. Accordingly, the second-highest score was found to be the item that says heads of schools can be trusted with confidential information (85.10%). So, heads of schools were found to be trustworthy in such a way that they cannot steal school's resources did not hurt someone's career because of a grudge (85.10%) nor they were hypocrite (85.10%).

Similarly, the item that asks if the head of schools would withhold information or constructive feedback because he/she wants someone to fail was the third important attribute of integrity with a frequency of 84.20%. Other items which scored highest frequencies and considered important attributes of integrity in Mbulu district include: would spread rumours or gossip to try to hurt people or the organization (84.20%), is rude or uncivil to co-workers (81.70%), shows unfair favouritisms toward some people (80.70%), would engage in sabotage of the organization (82.60%), likes to bend the rules (78.80%) and would make trouble for someone who got on his or her bad side (78.20%).

In case of the items which scored the lowest frequencies, Table 3.1 shows that item which says the heads of schools' ridicule people for their mistakes scored the lowest frequency of 30.20%. This means that heads of schools did not mentor and advise teachers when they make mistakes so that they cannot repeat similar mistakes in the future. Thus, the item was found to be the least important attribute of integrity possessed and practiced by the heads of schools in Mbulu district. Other attributes/items which were less important and less possessed and practiced by heads of schools in Mbulu district were; would try to take credit for other people's ideas (57.90%), enjoys turning down staff's requests (60.40%), would lie to me (65.30%) and has a high moral standard (64.80%).

Furthermore, the mean and standard deviation were calculated to ascertain data variability and reliability. The results in Table 3.2 indicate that the item which says the head of school cannot be trusted with confidential information scored the highest average of 3.9 (SD=1.9). This item has little dispersion and variability around the mean of the data set, on average. So the values in the statistical data set are close to the mean of a sample population. Similarly, the item that asks if the head of school has poor moral standard averaged 3.62 (SD=1.46) signifying that data variability around the mean is very small. Besides, the item which asks whether the head of school try to take credit for other person's ideas averaged 2.42 (SD=1.35). This item also possesses consistency data.

However, according to Al-Saleh and Yousif (2009:196), the items which showed high variability around the mean of data set they just reflect a large amount of variation in the group that is being studied. A small standard deviation can be a goal in certain situations where the results are restricted, but in situations where one just observes and record data; a large standard deviation is not necessarily a bad thing (Rumsey, 2016).

According to scholars such as Ojo (2011), Lumpkin, Claxton and Wilson (2014), Goolamally and Ahmad (2014) and Duggar, (2015), the HoS with the attribute of integrity are trustworthy, sincere, transparent, just and, as much as possible, show congruence between their feelings, thoughts,

9

actions and words. Besides, covers personal qualities such as self-respect, loyalty, and honesty towards oneself and staff and other stakeholders, do as they say, mentor their followers, have high moral values, not arrogant, not egoistic, courteous and respectful towards others. Thus, based on those qualities of effective secondary school leaders, in this study the 30 integrity constructs (items) were grouped into six categories of integrity attributes namely; trust, teamwork, sincere (not a hypocrite), altruistic (not selfish), not vindictive or arrogant and just (no favouritism).

In this study, the results revealed that head of schools (HoS) were trustworthy as they could not lie to teachers about important work-related information or engage in a sabotage plan against the school or even steal from the school. It was found out that HoS had a high moral standard such that he/she cannot bend the organization rules for personal gains, spread false rumours and gossips, blackmail staff or falsify records to help his/her career on the expense of the others.

The findings were corroborated and validated by key informants during a semi-structured interview. They reported that HoS can be trusted even with confident information. Moreover, as leaders, they understand the gravity of confidentiality of the information and the severity of punishment if they leaked confident information relating to work to other people/staff that are not entitled to its access. In a similar capacity, they can also contain and protect even social confident information regarding co-workers and people in the community he/she lives. During a semi-structured interview with the education officer, he had these to say:

"Yeah, the heads of schools are trustworthy people and very cooperative, enthusiastic, humble and their participation in different school activities is invaluable..., however, challenges always are there... some heads of school are inexperienced thus impede school and students' academic performance... you know headmaster's leadership skills are essential for effective school management and control which are associated with students' academic performance"

Harper (2017) argued that trust stands as the base foundation for which all leadership capabilities stem from. Similarly, in their meta-analysis Dirks and Skarlicki (2004) maintained that trust in leaders has been linked to positive job attitudes, organizational justice, psychological contracts, and effectiveness in terms of communication, organizational relationships, and conflict management. Empirical studies by Dirks and Ferrin (2002), Connell *et al.* (2003) and Costa (2003) have shown that having trust in one's leader, has been tied to desirable performance outcomes. Even though trustworthiness is an important attribute, the reality is leaders may be falling short in this character. According to Scott (2014), 45 percent of employees say a lack of trust in leadership is the biggest issue impacting work performance. A recent article by Randy (2016) stated that surveys and studies point to worsening levels of trust in leadership and organizations. The report states only 40 percent of employees have a high level of trust in their management and organization and 25 percent the lowest trust to their bosses and senior leaders.

Accordingly, in this study, three participants (teachers) lamented that their HoS were not to be trusted because of the behaviour they had demonstrated. However, the level of trust in selected secondary schools of Mbulu district was relatively higher than reported by the previous studies (Scott, 2014; Randy, 2016). Of the three teachers, the first one criticized the HoS where he works for rejecting or deprived him of his eligibility and right to live in the schoolhouse and instead a new female teacher was favoured as she was of the same ethnic with HoS. The second teacher bitterly explained the incidence of his request to go for further study was rejected while a very junior female teacher was approved by HoS. The other teacher complained that the head of his school is hypocrite, gossiper, and liar, cruel, separatist and evil who cannot be trusted at all. One teacher in FGD narrated the following:

"The head of my school likes some people than others and likes to be recognized for other people's efforts...not a hypocrite but you cannot trust her completely, low moral standard and lacks essential leadership qualities"

Another teacher sadly said that:

"The head of my school is not a good person; I had requested to go for further studies but keep rejecting my request while accepted a request of very junior staff. I went to DEO and REO to get help but it turned out that my head of school had already communicated with these officers about my requests and the rejections... they didn't help me. Staffs of opposite sex and teachers of his ethnic enjoy favours from the head of school. If I made a small mistake (and other unfavourable staffs) head of school would speak of it for a whole month... for sure there is NO integrity in that leadership"

It has been long and widely been believed that a leader with teamwork spirit or qualities is expected to produce quality results (Scarnati, 2001; Tarricone and Luca, 2002; Goyette, 2016). Teamwork of teachers is an important strategy to realize educational goals of the country (Emmanuel, 2015). Schools consist of members who should work as a team for the improvement of the school by utilizing the available resources (Babyegeya, 2002).

In the current study, the results revealed that HoS possessed teamwork qualities to a large extent. To ascertain this, the study found out that HoS were interested in tasks that didn't bring them personal glory and recognition but the responsible team. Thus, it was revealed that the HoS were team players and collaborative as they involved other teachers and staffs in decision-making process for planning, implementation, and evaluation of school projects. Hence, according to them (surveyed teachers), the involvement of teachers and staffs motivates them as it brings a sense of project ownership and thus encourages and inspires them to do their work effectively; as a result, improve school and students' academic performance.

Therefore, to affirm heads of schools' team-work spirit, the 202 surveyed teachers revealed that HoS do cooperate with all staffs to solve the problems and advise them on how best they can conduct their businesses without violating schools' guidelines and overall national level employment by-laws, policy, and guidelines which are given periodically. However, teachers and other officials in FGD and a semi-structured interview with key informants had mixed views. Some participants opposed HoS possess teamwork qualities while others were in favour.

Contrary to this study, Emmanuel (2015) revealed that teamwork of teachers in Tanzania was very weak in academic and work-related matters such as teaching and learning but strong and effective in social matters such as ceremonies and sports. According to Maina (2010), academic improvement of the students by raising performance is a major product of the teachers' teamwork. Maina (2010) has indicated that the performance increases when the school leader builds a teamwork spirit on teachers. Primrose and Chrispen (2013) have observed that teachers' teamwork improves students' academic improvement in schools. Moreover, the findings from the study carried out by Kilewo (2014) in Tanzania shows that teamwork influences students' academic performance. Also, Llah (2010), show that the spirit of teamwork of teachers makes the school perform well.

To be trusted, principals must also be honest in their interactions with teachers (Tschannen-Moran and Hoy, 1998). Honest behavior is anchored in moral principles and is cultivated through

12

behaviors that demonstrate the integrity of character (Tschannen-Moran Gareis, 2015a. In general, the study found that HoS were the problem solver and conflict mediator among school staff, or among staff and students, or students themselves. The findings declared that HoS were in the front line to solve problems and mediate conflicts among staffs, students and community in general. FGD, participants corroborated the findings. Similarly, Julius (2014) found that the majority of teachers at the Meru County in Kenya were honest and hard working. He further postulated that honest of teachers is a positive attitude on pupils' academic performance.

Moreover, another teacher happily added that:

"Our head of school is keen, smart and organized... always is working to fulfil both school goal and the goals given by the LGA and MOEVT. She has a very high moral standard and likes to recognize teachers for their efforts. She despises hypocrites and lazy teachers"

Honesty means to be free from deceit and fraud, to be open and above board in your transactions, and to be fair and just in how you treat others. Honest people do not say things they know are not true, they do not take things of value that belong to others, they do not knowingly give false impressions, and they follow the rules they have agreed to accept (Cherrington, David, and Cherrington, Owen, 1993). Also, Hsieh (2002) defined honesty as the virtue of refusing to fake the facts of reality, commitment to the facts is simply rationality.

Therefore, the general view of the study based on the descriptive findings, depict that HoS had demonstrated a high degree of integrity. It was revealed that they treat all the teachers and staffs equally with respect and cooperation. Heads of schools involve teachers and no-teaching staffs in the decision-making process such as teaching allocation, conflict resolution, extracurricular activities and disciplining staffs and students. With this level of integrity Mbulu secondary school education is expected to rise soon.

Moreover, researches on school management have found that schools which attained a high rate of academic success were led by heads of schools with effective leadership qualities such as integrity (Quick and Normore, 2004; Drysdale, Goode and Gurr, 2009; Ojo, 2011; Goolamally and Ahmad, 2014; Lumpkin, Claxton land Wilson, 2014). In their study, Goolamally and Ahmad (2014) identified integrity among the five most important leadership attributes which a school leader must possess to make a school excellent. Kor (2010) refers to heads of schools that maintain personal integrity and lead with moral purpose as "values-driven" leaders. With this kind of school heads, the school's administration and students' academic performance are expected to improve. However, in Tanzanian context multitude of factors hinders the expectations.

The findings of the study concur with Preetika and Priti (2013) study conducted in India which revealed that integrity among school leaders was observed to positively influence teachers' satisfaction with the job which in turn motivated teachers to teach students and improved students' academic performance. Not only that but also Kariuk (2006) found out a positive significant relationship between school leadership integrity and academic performance in Kenya. Moreover, in their study, Goolamally and Ahmad (2014) identified integrity among the five most important leadership attributes which a school leader must possess to make a school and students' academic performance excellent. Thus, they concluded that a school leader's integrity was positively influencing the academic performance of students. This study, therefore, suggests that there is a positive and significant relationship between secondary school leaders' integrity and students' academic performance in Mbulu district.

4. CONCLUSION

The study carried out to 202 teachers to provide evidence of the existence and application of integrity, attributes of heads of schools and influences the student academic performance in Mbulu district. The findings of the study overwhelmingly support the assumptions that, integrity attributes significantly influence students' academic performance. It is recommended that induction and in-service training on leadership behaviour, management skills, instructional leadership and professional development for the newly appointed heads of school to equip the immature heads in their administrative and management duties are of paramount as it reinforces leadership attributes.

5. TABLES AND FIGURES

In this section, the researcher presents results for the assessment of the influence of integrity attribute of the heads of schools on the students' academic performance in selected secondary schools in Mbulu district. Table 3.1 and 3.2 summarises frequencies and percentages distribution of the 30 items of integrity to show the extent of application of integrity attribute on school leadership and its impact on students' academic performance in Mbulu district as discussed above (section 3.0 Findings and discussion).

Table 3.1: Frequency Distribution of Integrity Indicators (N=202)

	Indicator	SDA N(%)	DA N(%)	NT N(%)	AG N(%)	SA N(%)
1	Puts personal interests ahead of organisation's	109(54.00)	29(14.40)	17(08.40)	36(17.80)	11(05.40)
2	Would risk other people to protect himself or herself in works matters.	117(57.90)	26(12.90)	19(09.40)	35(17.30)	05(02.50)
3	Enjoys turning down staff's requests	92(45.50)	30(14.90)	32(15.80)	31(15.30)	17(08.40)
4	Deliberately fuels conflict between other people	125(61.90)	10(08.90)	15(07.40)	32(15.80)	12(05.90)
5	Would blackmail an employee if she/he thought could get away with	110(54.50)	28(13.90)	27(13.4)	21(10.40)	16(07.90)
6	Would deliberately exaggerate peoples mistake to make them look bad to others	128(63.40)	20(09.90)	23(11.40)	26(12.90)	05(02.50)
7	Would treat some people better if they were of other sex or belonged to same ethnic group	106(52.50)	27(13.40)	16(07.90)	31(15.30)	22(10.90)
8	Ridicules people for their mistakes	43(21.30)	18(08.90)	18(08.90)	58(28.70)	64(31.70)
9	Can be trusted with confident information	159(78.70)	13(06.40)	16(07.90)	06(03.00)	08(04.00)
10	Would lie to me	101(50.00)	31(15.30)	34(16.80)	25(12.40)	11(05.40)
11	Is evil	131(64.90)	19(09.40)	26(12.90)	17(08.40)	09(04.50)
12	Is not interested in task that don't bring him/her personal glory or recognition	94(46.50)	40(19.80)	26(12.90)	26(12.90)	16(07.90)
13	Would violate organizational policy and then expect others to cover for him or her	138(60.30)	22(10.90)	20(09.90)	13(06.40)	09(04.50)

15

No.	Statement				
14	Would allow someone else to be blamed for his or her mistake	121(59.90)	28(13.90)	27(13.40)	16(07.90)	10(05.00)
15	Would deliberately not answer email, telephone /message to cause problems for someone else.	122(60.40)	32(15.80)	15(07.40)	18(08.90)	15(07.40)
16	Would make trouble for someone who got on his or her bad side	107(53.00)	51(25.20)	23(11.40)	17(08.40)	04(02.00)
17	Would engage in sabotage of the organization	134(66.30)	33(16.30)	22(10.90)	06(03.00)	07(03.50)
18	Would deliberately distort what other people say	120(59.40)	33(16.30)	21(10.40)	23(11.40)	05(02.50)
19	Is hypocrite	154(76.20)	18(08.90)	16(07.90)	09(04.50)	05(02.50)
20	Is vindictive	118(58.40)	32(15.80)	25(12.40)	16(07.90)	11(05.40)
21	Would try to take credit for other people's ideas	71(35.10)	46(22.80)	30(14.90)	39(19.30)	16(07.90)
22	Likes to bend the rules	131(64.90)	28(13.90)	19(09.40)	15(07.40)	09(04.50)
23	Would withhold information or constructive feedback because he/she wants someone to fail	140(69.30)	30(14.90)	18(08.90)	12(05.90)	02(01.00)
24	Would spread rumours or gossip to try to hurt people or the organization	146(72.30)	24(11.90)	18(08.90)	07(03.50)	07(03.50)
25	Is rude or uncivil to co workers	131(64.90)	34(16.80)	21(10.40)	11(05.40)	05(02.50)
26	Would hurt someone's career because of grudge	141(69.80)	31(15.30)	15(07.40)	09(04.50)	06(03.00)
27	Shows unfair favouritisms toward some people	129(63.90)	34(16.80)	20(09.90)	10(05.00)	09(04.50)
28	Would steal from the organization	151(74.80)	22(10.90)	12(05.90)	13(06.40)	04(02.00)
29	Would falsify records if it would help his/her work situation	125(61.90)	26(12.90)	22(10.90)	20(09.90)	09(04.50)
30	Has a high moral standard	34(16.80)	12(05.90)	25(12.40)	56(27.70)	75(37.10)

Source: Field Data 2019

Table 3.2: Mean and Std Deviation of Integrity Leadership Attribute Items (N=202)

S/N	Item/Statement	N	Mean	Std. Deviation
1	Puts his or her interests ahead of the organizations	202	2.06	1.353
2	Would risk other people to protect him or herself in works matters	202	1.94	1.262
3	Enjoys turning down requests	202	2.26	1.388
4	Deliberately fuels conflict between other people	202	1.95	1.367
5	Blackmail an employee if she or he thought she or he could get away with	202	2.03	1.347
6	Deliberately exaggerate peoples mistakes to make them look bad to others	202	1.81	1.207
7	Treat some people better if they were of the other sex or belonged	201	2.17	1.464
8	Ridicules people for mistakes	202	2.08	1.287
9	Cannot be trusted with confidential information	202	3.88	1.898
10	Would lie to me	202	1.78	1.214
11	Is evil	202	1.47	1.033
12	Is not interested in the task that doesn't bring personal glory or recognition	202	2.16	1.344
13	Do things that violate the organizational policy and expect others to cover for him/her	202	1.68	1.159
14	Would allow someone else to be blamed for his or her mistakes	202	1.84	1.215
15	Deliberately avoid responding to email, telephone, or other communication means	202	1.87	1.302
16	Make trouble for someone who got on his or her bad side	202	1.81	1.062
17	Engage in sabotage against the organization	202	1.61	1.027
18	Deliberately distort what other people say	202	1.81	1.161
19	Is hypocrite	202	1.48	.989
20	Is vindictive	202	1.86	1.226
21	Try to take credit for other people's ideas	202	2.42	1.348
22	Likes to bend the rules	202	1.73	1.172
23	Withhold information or constructive feedback as he/she wants someone to fail	202	1.54	.952
24	Would spread rumours or gossip to try to hurt people or organization	202	1.54	1.027
25	Is rude or uncivil to co-workers	202	1.64	1.033
26	Try to hurt someone's career because of grudge	202	1.55	1.012
27	Shows unfair favouritism towards some people	202	1.69	1.117
28	Would steal from the organization	202	1.50	.999
29	Would falsify records if it would help his or her work situation	202	1.82	1.225
30	Has a poor moral standard	202	3.62	1.455

Source: Field Data 2019

6. DISCLOSURE OF CONFLICT OF INTEREST

The findings revealed in this study is only merely research study, does not reflect the weakness of individual person, rather the education institutions particularly the selected secondary schools for the purpose of improving the student academic performance. And the data collected were highly observed confidentialities and were used for academic purposes only. Should any person relate the information's obtained here into the report, with any person or group of people, should not be treated as crime since all ethical procedures regarding academics were followed thoroughly well?

7. ACKNOWLEDGEMENT

The support and assistance of my supervisors' Dr Cosmas B.M. Haule and Dr Joseph J. Magali were invaluable to the work. I truly, appreciate the encouragement and support of my supervisors, their contributions and encouragement to learning activities was quite valuable as they guided me without getting tired. I also thank my staff workers in my District commissioner office particularly to support my work whenever they were required either through fulfilling my duties or academic contributions. I would like to thank too, the Manyara regional Commissioner Hon. Alexander Pastory Mnyeti for his encouragement and support of permission whenever required to travel for academic purposes. I really enjoyed learning and growing alongside of each of them, their humour and remarkable insight made every learning interesting and engaging.

8. REFERENCES

Aaker, D.A., Kumar, V., and Day, G.S. (2001). *Marketing research*. New York, USA: John Wiley and Sons Inc. Page 751

Abdullah et al (2012). The need to explore emotional intelligence (EI) skills amongst Malaysian public librarians. Proceedings of international business information management (IBIM) May 2012, INstabul ISSN 978-0-98214897-6

Abubakar, U. (2018). The difference between education and academics (Blog post). Accessed from https://tutors.com.ng/2018/08/02/the-difference-between-education-and-academics/html

Ache Health Care. (2018). *Health care leader's alliance and the college of healthy executives' competencies assessment tool*. USA. Author.

Adam, J. and Kamuzora, F. (2008). *Research methods for business and social studies*. Morogoro, Tanzania: Mzumbe Book Project.

Adebayo, F.A. (2009). Parents' preference for private secondary schools in Nigeria. Kamla-Raj 2009. *International Journal of Education Science, 1(1), 1-6*

Adeleye, J.O. (2017). Pragmatism and its implications on teaching and learning in Nigerian schools. *Research Highlights in Education and Science*, Page 2-6

Adeyemi, O. T. (2013). Principal's leadership styles and student academic performance in secondary schools in Ekiti State, Nigeria. *International Journal of Academic Research in Progressive Education and Development*. 2(1), 187-198

Afeli, (2017). *Regional workshop on national learning assessment systems in Sub-Saharan Africa: Knowledge sharing and needs assessment*. Paper presented at the UNESCO and TALENT Workshop on National Learning Assessment Systems in Dakar, Senegal from 6th to 8th December, 2017.

Ahmed, J.U. (2010). Documentary research method: New dimensions. *Indus Journal of Management and Social Sciences*, 4(1), 1-14

Ahmed, S. (2009). Statistical methods for sample surveys (140.640): Introduction to sampling method (Lecture). University of John Hopkins.

Ahmet, AVCI. (2016). Effect of leadership styles of school principals on organizational citizenship behaviours. *Educational Research and Reviews*, 11(11), 1008-1024

20

Ajayi, V.O. (2017). *Primary sources of data and secondary sources of data; Distinguish between primary sources of data and secondary sources of data.* Benue State University, Makurdi. Faculty of Education Department of Curriculum And Teaching

Akaranga, S.I. and Makau, B.K. (2016). Ethical considerations and their applications to research: a Case of the University of Nairobi. *Journal of Educational Policy and Entrepreneurial Research,* 3(12), 1-91.

Akiri, (2017). Lecturer's professional competency and student academic performance, in Indonesia Higher Education. *International Journal of Human Resources Studies,* 7 (1).

Akiri, A.A. (2013). Effects of teachers' effectiveness on students' academic performance in public secondary schools; Delta State – Nigeria. *Journal of Educational and Social Research,* 3(3)

Aline, I. and Ramkumar, S. (2018). Leaders are not born, they are made. *International Journal of Applied Research,* 4(5), 94-96

Al-Karasneh, S. and Jubran, A. (2013). Classroom leadership and creativity: A study of social studies and islamic education teachers in Jordan. *Creative Education,* 4(10)

Alkarni, A. (2015). Problems which may challenge the ability of secondary school head teachers in the City of Tabuk to lead their schools professionally. *ARECLS,* 11, 55-74.

Allen, N., Grigsby, B. and Peters, M.L. (2015). Does leadership matter? Examining the relationship among transformational leadership, school climate, and student achievement. *NCPEA International Journal of Educational Leadership Preparation,* 10(2)

Allport, G. W., and Odbert, H. S. (1936). Trait names. A psycho-lexical study. *Psychological monographs,* 47, pp 211.

Almalki, S. (2016). Integrating quantitative and qualitative data in mixed methods research—challenges and benefits. *Journal of Education and Learning;* 5(3)

Al-Saleh, M.F. and Yousif, A.E. (2009). Properties of the Standard Deviation that are rarely mentioned in classrooms. *Austrian Journal of Statistics,* 38(3), 193–202

Alvaro, C., and Maria, G. (2017). *Does school leadership affect student academic achievement?* Fundació Jaume Bofill, Ivàlua.

Amuche, C.I. and Saleh, D.A. (2013). Principals managerial competence asa correlate of students' academic performance in Ecwa secondary schools in North Central Nigeria. *Journal of Education and Practice,* 4(4).

Annie, W., Howard, W.S. and Mildred, M. (1996). Achievement and ability tests: Definition of the domain. Educational Measurement 2, University Press of America, pages 2–5.

Appoline, A.T. (2015). *Motivational strategies used by principals in the management of schools. The Case of some selected secondary schools in the Fako division of the Southwest region of Cameroon.* Master's Thesis in Education, Department of Education, University of Jyvaskyla.

Ardichvili, A., Dag, K.N. and Manderscheid, S. (2016). Leadership development: Current and emerging models and practices. *Advances in Developing Human Resources*, 18(3), 275-285.

Arshad M., Zaidi, S.M.I.H and Mahmood K. (2015). Self-Esteem and academic performance among university students. *Journal of Education and Practice*, 6(1), 156-162

Asimaki A., and Vergidis K. D. (2013). Detecting the gender dimension of the choice of the teaching profession prior to the economic crisis and imf (international monetary fund) memorandum in Greece: A case study. *International Educational Studies*, 6(4), 140–153.

Avery, G.C. (2004) *Understanding leadership: Paradigms and cases.* London: Sage.

Awiti, F. S. (2013). *Management strategies of teachers turn over in Ilala municipal.* A Dissertation Submitted for Partial Fulfilment of the Requirements for the Award of the Degree of Masters of Science in Human Resources Management of Mzumbe University.

Ayeni, A. J. (2005). *The effect of principals' leadership styles on motivation of teachers for job performance in secondary schools in Akure South local government.* A Dissertation Submitted to the Department of Educational Administration and Planning for Partial Fulfilment of Award of Masters Art in Education of Obafemi Awolowo University, Ile-Ife.

Azaliwa, E.A and Casmir, A. (2016). A comparative study of teachers' motivation on work performance in selected public and private secondary schools in Kilimanjaro region, Tanzania. *International Journal of Education and Research. 4(6)*, 583-600

Babajani, J. (2008). The analysis theatrical and legal basis of 2008 budgeting new approach of view accountability, *Hesabdar*, 194, 4-5

Babajani, J. (2010). Challenges of public sector financial reporting. *Hesabras*, 48, 96-97

Bahta, S.T. and Bauer, S. (2007). *Analysis of the determinants of market participation within the South African small-scale livestock sector.* Tropentag, October 9 -11, 2007, Witzenhausen: Utilisation of diversity in land use systems: Sustainable and organic approaches to meet human needs. Tropentag Paper.

Bailey, K.D. (1982). *Methods of social research* (2nd Ed.). New York: Free Press. 553 p

Balihar, S. (2007). Qualitative research methods: documentary research (Blog post). Accessed from http://uk.geocities.com/balihar_sanghera/qrmdocumentaryresearch.html

Balliro, M.J. (2018). *The new sincerity in American literature.* A dissertation submitted in partial fulfilment of the requirements for the Degree of Doctor of Philosophy in English of University of Rhode Island

Bandura, A. (1997). *Self-efficacy: The exercise of control.* New York: W.H Freeman and Company

Baron, R.M., and d Kenny, D.A. (1986). The moderator–mediator variable distinction in social psychological research: Conceptual, strategic, and statistical considerations. *Journal of Personality and Social Psychology,* Volume 51(6), 1173–1182

Barth, R.S. (2009). *Improve schools from within: Teachers, parents, and principles can make a difference.* San Francisco, CA: Jossey-Bas.

Bass B. M., (1990). *Bass and Stogdills handbook of leadership. theory research and managerial application.* New York: Free Press.

Baum, D.R. and Riley, I. (2018). The relative effectiveness of private and public schools: evidence from Kenya. *An International Journal of Research, Policy and Practice.*

Baxter, and Jack, (2008). Qualitative case study methodology: Study design and implementation for novice researchers. *The Qualitative Report,* 1(4), 554-559.

Bedi, A. S., and Garg, A. (2000). The Effectiveness of private versus public schools: The C\case of Indonesia. *Journal of Development Economics,* 61(2), 463-494.

Begna, T.N. (2017). Public schools and private schools in Ethiopia: Partners in national development? *International Journal of Humanities Social Sciences and Education, 4(2), 100-111*

Bennel, P. and Mukyanuzi, F. (2005). *Is there a teacher motivation crisis in Tanzania?* Research Report Fund. Dar es Salaam: HR-Consult.

Bennell, P. (2004). *Teacher motivation and incentives in Sub -Saharan Africa and Asia.* Brighton: Knowledge and Skills for Development

Bennis, W. G., and Naus, B. (2003). *Leaders: The strategies for taking charge.* New York: Harper and Row.

Bernardo, A. B. I., Ganotice, F.A. and King, R.B. (2014). Motivation gap and achievement gap between public and private high schools in the Philippines. *The Asia-Pacific Education Researcher,* 24(4).

Bill, M. (2008). *The leadership challenge in improving learning in schools.* Australia: Australia Council for Educational Research,

Black, P.J., Woodworth, M. and Porter, S. (2014). The big bad wolf? The relation between the dark triad and the interpersonal assessment of vulnerability. *Personality and Individual Differences,* 67, 52-56.

Blanche, M. T., Durrheim, K. and Painter, D. (2006). *Research in practice: Applied methods for the social sciences.* Juta and Company Ltd.

Bleiklie, I. and Michelsen, S. (2013). Comparing higher education policies in Europe: Structures and reform outputs in eight countries', *Higher Education,* 65, 113–133.

Bleiklie, I., Enders, J., Lepori, B. and C. Musselin (2011). New public management, network governance and the university as a changing professional organization', in T. Christensen and P. Laegreid (eds) *The Ashgate Research Companion to New Public Management,* (pp. 161–176) (Farnham: Ashgate).

Bloor, M., Frankland, J., Thomas, M., and Robson, K. (2001). *Focus groups in social research.* London, Thousand Oaks -CA: Sage Publications Inc.

Bolat O.İ, Bolat T, and Seymen O.A (2009). Güçlendirici lider davranışları ve örgütsel vatandaşlık davranışı arasındaki ilişkinin sosyal mübadele kuramından hareketle incelenmesi. Balıkesir Üniversitesi Sosyal Bilimler Enstitüsü Dergisi 12(21), 215-239.

Boniface, R., (2016). *Teachers' retention in Tanzanian remote secondary schools: Exploring perceived challenges and support.* Doctoral dissertation, Department of Education, Linnaeus University, Sweden.

Bowen, G. A. (2009). Document analysis as a qualitative research method. *Qualitative Research Journal,* 9(2), 27-40. doi:10.3316/QRJ0902027

Braun, V. and Clarke, V. (2006) Using thematic analysis in psychology. *Qualitative Research in Psychology,* 3 (2), 77-101.

Burns, N., and Grove, S. K. (2003). T*he practice of Nursing Research: Conduct, critique and utilization.* Philadelphia: W. Saunders.

Byabato,S., and Kisamo, K. (2014). Implementation of school based continuous assessment in Tanzania ordinary secondary schools and its implications on the quality of education. *Developing Country Studies,* 4(6)

Campanelli, P. (2008). Testing survey questions. In E.D. De Leeuw, J.J. Hox, and D.A. Dillman (Eds), *International Handbook of Survey Methodology,* New York: Lawrence Erlbaum Associates

Cardoso, S., Carvalho, T. and Santiago, R. (2011). From students to consumers: Reflections on the marketisation of Portuguese higher education', *European Journal of Education*, 46(2), 271-284.

Caspar, R., Peytcheva, E., Yan, Y., Lee, S., Liu, M. and Hu, M. (2016). Pretesting Cross-cultural survey guidelines. CC56

Ceil, C., and Sykes, J. (2012). *Women in leadership*. New York: Social Science Electronic Publishing Inc. Retrieved November 28, 2015, from http://ssrn.com/abstract=2051415

Cerit, Y. (2009). The effects of servant leadership behaviours of school principals on teachers' job satisfaction. *Educational Management Administration and Leadership* 37(5), 600–623

Chaudhary, A.K. and Israel, G.D. (2014). The Savvy survey #8: Pilot testing and pretesting questionnaires. IFAS extension, University of Florida

Cheng, Y.C and Townsend, T. (2000). Educational change and development in the Asian Pacific region: trends and issues, In T. Townsend and Y.C. Cheng (Eds). *Educational change and development in the Asia-Pacific region: Challenges for the future*, Rotterdam: Swets and Zeitlinger.

Cherrington, David J. and J. Owen, Cherrington (1993). Understanding honesty. *Internal Auditor*, *pp* 29-35.

Cherry, K. (2016). *What is the trait theory of leadership?* Retrieved from https://www.verywell.com/what-is-the-trait-theory-of-leadership-2795322

Cherry, K. (2019). *How extroversion in personality influences behaviour.* Accessed from https://www.verywellmind.com/what-is-extroversion-2795994

Cho, J., and Trent, A. (2006). Validity in qualitative research revisited. *Qualitative Research*, 6(3), 319-340.

Chrzanowska, J. (2002). *Interviewing groups and individuals in qualitative market research* (Vol. 2). London: Sage. 176 p

Churchil, G.A. and Iacobucci, D. (2005). Marketing research: Methodological foundation (9th Ed.). USA: Thomson South-Western

Churchill, G. A. (1996). *Basic marketing research (3rd Ed.)*, Fort Worth, TX: The Dryden Press

Clarke, J., and Wood, D. (2001). New public management and development: The case of public service reform in Tanzania and Uganda. In McCourt, W., and Minongue, M., (Eds.), *the Internationalization of public management: Reinventing the Third World State*. Cheltenham, Edward Elgar.

Clarke, V., and Braun, V. (2013). Teaching thematic analysis: Overcoming challenges and developing strategies for effective learning. *Psychologist, 26*(2), 120-123.

Cohen, L., Manion, L., and Marrison, K. (2007). *Research methods in education (6th edition).* London: Routledge Taylor and Francis group. 638 p.

Commission Malaysia.

Conger J.A., and Kanungo R.N, (1987). Charismatic leadership in organization perceived behavioural –attributes and their measurement. *A Journal of Organizational Behavioural,* 15, 439-452.

Conroy, R.M. (2016). The RCSI sample size handbook: A rough guide

Cortina, J.M. (1993). What is coefficient Alpha? An examination of theory and applications. *Journal of Applied Psychology,* 78(1), 98-104

Creswell, J. W. (2007). *Qualitative inquiry and research design: Choosing among five approaches (2nd ed.).* Thousand Oaks, CA, US: Sage

Creswell, J. W. (2014). *Research design: Qualitative, quantitative, and mixed methods approaches.* Sage. 342 p.

Creswell, J. W., and Plano Clark, V. L. (2011). *Designing and conducting mixed methods research* (2nd ed.). London: Sage.

Creswell, J. W., Fetters, M. D. and Ivankova, N. V. (2004). Designing a Mixed methods study in primary care. *The Annals of Family Medicine, 2*(1), 7-12.

Creswell, J.W. (2009) *Research design: qualitative, quantitative, and mixed methods approaches* (3rd Ed.). Thousand Oaks, CA: Sage.

Crossman, A., and Harris, P. (2006). Job satisfaction of secondary school teachers. *Educational Management and Leadership, 34(1),* 29-46.

Crow, G. (2001). School leader preparation: A short review of the knowledge base. National College for School Leadership. Available at http://www.ncsl.org.uk/mediastore/image2/randd-gary-crow-paper.pdf

Cuthill, M. (2002). Exploratory research: citizen participation, local government and sustainable development in Australia. *Sustainable Development,* 10, 79-89.

Dang, V. H. (2015). A mixed method approach enabling the triangulation technique: A case study in Vietnam. *World Journal of Social Science,* (2)2

Daniel, R. (2003). *The Role of school leadership on student achievement.* Luxemburg, Italy.

Gbollie, C. and Keamu, H.P. (2017). Student academic performance: The role of motivation, strategies, and perceived factors hindering Liberian junior and senior high school students learning. *Education Research International*, Volume 2017, Article ID 1789084, 11 pages

Hidalgo (2002) .Integrity retrieved from http//www.webweever.com/integrity.htm

Mohd Najib(2009), I Malaysia concept can earn the country respect, retrieved from: http//www.1malaysia.com.org/index

Polit D.F and Beck C.T (2010). Generalization in quantitative and qualitative research: Myths and strategies. International journal of nursing studies, 47(11) 1451-1453

Risik et al 920110, A cross-cultural examination of the endorsement of ethical leadership, journal of Business Ethics 63(4), 345-359

Salmon D. And Rickby C(2012), City of one. A quantitative study examining the participation of young people in care in a theatre and music initiative, children and society.

Shek D.(2012), Evaluation of a positive youth development program based on the repertory and test. The scientific journal world journal 2012, 1-12.

Sidek (2009), Public services people first, performance now, paper presented at public service

YOUR KNOWLEDGE HAS VALUE

- We will publish your bachelor's and master's thesis, essays and papers

- Your own eBook and book - sold worldwide in all relevant shops

- Earn money with each sale

Upload your text at www.GRIN.com and publish for free